Quick
&
easy

Freshwater
Aquarium Setup
& Care

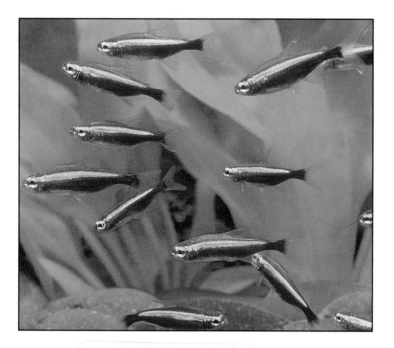

D0111270

Quick & Easy Freshwater Aquarium Setup & Care

Project Team
Editor: Brian M. Scott
Copy Editor: Carl Schutt
Design: Patricia Escabi
Series Design: Mary Ann Kahn

T.F.H. Publications
President/CEO: Glen S. Axelrod
Executive Vice President: Mark E. Johnson
Publisher: Christopher T. Reggio
Production Manager: Kathy Bontz

T.F.H. Publications, Inc.
One TFH Plaza
Third and Union Avenues
Neptune City, NJ 07753

Library of Congress Cataloging-In-Publication Data
Quick & easy freshwater aquarium set-up & care / TFH staff.
p. cm.
Includes bibliographical references.
ISBN 0-7938-1042-6 (alk. paper)
1.   Aquariums. I. Title: Quick and easy freshwater aquarium set-up and care. II.
T.F.H. Publications, Inc.
SF457.3Q85 2005
639.34-dc22
2005011904

This book has been published with the intent to provide accurate and authoritative information
in regard to the subject matter within. While every precaution has been taken in preparation of
this book, the author and publisher expressly disclaim responsibility for any errors, omissions, or
adverse effects arising from the use or application of the information contained herein. The techniques and suggestions are used at the reader's discretion and are not to be considered a sub-
stitute for veterinary care. If you suspect a medical problem, consult your veterinarian.

The Leader in Responsible Animal Care for over 50 years.
www.tfhpublications.com

Table of Contents

Introduction to Aquariums

So, this is your first aquarium! Certainly, you want every-thing to go smoothly with no hitches, right? Well, you are on the right track, since you are taking the time to read this book. By the time you finish reading it, you will have learned how to successfully set up your aquarium tank. Read this material from cover to cover, and then make your decisions about equipment and design based on the knowledge that you have gained. Educating yourself about aquarium keeping before you buy any equipment or fish will save you money and time in the long run. Hopefully, your knowledge gained will save some fishes' lives, too. One more thing: If you have tried aquarium keeping before without success, this book will surely send you on your way to a proper start.

First, let's explore your motivation for wanting an aquarium. Perhaps you recently visited a friend and saw his tank. It may have been a beautifully decorated exhibit replete with lush green plants, sleek pieces of driftwood, and magnificent, colorful, active fishes. You were envious and immediately wanted to rush out and buy a tank of your own. On the other hand, you might know someone who prefers a different sort of arrangement—nothing fancy, just plenty of fish with lots of interesting things going on that it glued you to the tank. It's better than television and a lot more interesting, too. It's even educational. Now, what's better than that?

Don't be frightened by the word "educational," for it aptly describes the benefits that can be derived from a novice fishkeeping experience. If you are a teacher, keep education in mind throughout each step of the set-up procedure; emphasize the fun involved (the education will take care of itself). If your aquarium is a class project, perhaps each student or a small group can be given specific duties such as selecting the equipment, setting up the tank, or choosing the fishes. A coordinated effort will result in success in all stages and produce the desired effect of an up-and-running aquarium.

Aquarium keeping can be a highly educational experience for both kids and adults.

Angelfish will be more at home in a dimly lit aquarium with slightly acidic water conditions.

There is always the chance that you are reading this book because you have received an aquarium as a gift. This is a thoughtful way for your friends or relatives to teach you the value of caring for living things. In each of us, there is an inborn urge to communicate with the world around us. Learning about fishes and their requirements will give you a good lesson in objectivity which will serve you well throughout life. For retirees, keeping an aquarium is a perfect full-time activity. It offers something to do, something to watch, and something to care for.

More so, keeping an aquarium is beneficial to one's health, too! Medical evidence supports the therapeutic value of caring for and watching fish swim in an aquarium; it lowers blood pressure and induces a general feeling of calmness and a sense of well-being. There is not much left in this world that can claim to reduce stress. Thank goodness for aquariums!

As you can see, the answer to the question, who can benefit from an aquarium? is that anyone, at any age, can find their own individual reason for setting up their first aquarium. It is just as easy for a youngster (recommended age is eight and above) as it is for an adult to keep an aquarium, as long as a few simple rules and precautions are followed.

Introduction to Aquariums 7

There are many types of aquariums designed to accommodate and maintain living organisms. The most popular type, especially with beginners, is the community tank. This implies that a variety of fishes are all living together in a relatively stable and harmonious environment. There are several types of community tanks. For example, one type is a community of fishes from one particular area. These aquariums are called "geographically correct" aquariums and serve to exhibit the diversity of fish life within a specific area. Within these are the "biotope aquariums" that replicate a specific environment within a geographical area. A good example of a biotope aquarium is one that replicates the soft, acidic waters of the Rio Negro in Brazil. Another common example is a biotope aquarium that simulates the rubble zone of Lake Malawi in Africa. As you gain experience in fishkeeping, you'll learn about many different biotopes that you can replicate as time goes on.

Many years ago when the aquarium hobby was young (1900-1940) there was a serious lack of equipment available to the tropical fish hobbyist. They were forced to improvise and make-do with what was available at the time. Everyone strived to create an environment within the tank that closely approximated conditions found in nature. Artificial means of filtration and aeration were sometimes scorned. Such a tank was referred to as a *balanced* aquarium. These were supposed to have a perfect balance of plants, fishes, and sometimes even freshwater invertebrates. The animals and plants would utilize, give off, and absorb equal quantities of oxygen and carbon dioxide. The water would remain "sweet," or purified, due to the natural filtration action of the live plants. Aquarists would brag that they had not changed the water for years.

In practice, the balanced aquarium was like Utopia, often strived for but rarely, if ever, achieved. A "modified" balanced community tank ("modified" meaning you are using equipment to mimic conditions of nature), on the other hand, can be set up and successfully maintained by virtually anyone. Essential component parts of such an aquarium include fishes, plants, and modern equipment.

Selecting & Outfitting Your Aquarium

Whaat size aquarium should you purchase? It depends, of course, on how much space is available and how much money you have to spend on it. The best size for an initial community tank is in the range of 20 to 30 gallons. There is a general rule of thumb that holds that the smaller the tank, the more difficult it is to properly maintain. This is true because the smaller the volume of water is, the more influenced it is by pollutants. Although the most popular size aquarium is the 10-gallon aquarium, it really is too small to function as a typical community tank. A 30-gallon aquarium is a good choice, but the cost factor must be considered. As a consumer, the size is up to you. You must be satisfied with your selection. While a 10-gallon aquarium is harder to maintain than a 20-gallon one, it is by no means difficult.

Selecting An Aquarium

If you have selected a 20-gallon tank, you will have the choice of a 20-gallon high or a 20-gallon long. The difference is obvious at first glance. The dimensions of a 20-gallon high are 24 inches long by 16 inches high by 12 inches wide. The dimensions of a 20-gallon long are 30 inches long by 12 inches high by 12 inches wide. So, you have the choice of a high tank versus a long tank. Whichever one you choose will affect all the contents of the aquarium. If you find yourself in a dilemma, you may take the easy way out by buying a 30-gallon tank. Its dimensions are 36 inches long by 16 inches high by 12 inches wide. With this tank you have both length and depth. By the way, the 20-gallon tank doesn't contain 20 gallons of water; it is just an approximation. A gallon of pure water weighs about 8.2 pounds. One cubic foot of water weighs 62.4 pounds. A 20-gallon long contains 2.2 cubic feet, or 18.7 gallons, when completely filled.

Be sure to carefully inspect your new aquarium before you fill it with water.

Aquarium Stands

You may have purchased a stand for your aquarium, or you may have a piece of furniture that will serve as one. Either way, the location of your tank is important. It should never be placed directly in a window, since too much light will cause the water to turn green with algae in a short time. Likewise, an area where people are constantly moving back and forth is unwise, since the activity may frighten the fish. Ideally, the base of the aquarium should be 30 inches from the floor, with a higher level being more practical than a lower one. Double-decker stands are fine as long as fish that do not frighten easily are placed in the bottom tank. A maximum of two hours of direct sunlight is beneficial. More exposure than that will overheat the water. The remainder of the light should be supplied by the bulb in the hood covering the tank.

Most aquariums are made of glass with molded plastic trim to give a finished look and to protect the edges of the glass (and the hands of the aquarist). The plastic trim may be wood grain, black, brown, or tan. Bernard Duke invented an all-glass tank with a stainless steel trim, but it has all but disappeared from the marketplace. A few firms make plastic tanks, but they are not as readily available as glass.

It is important that you carefully inspect the aquarium you decide to purchase. Check for cracks, pits, flaws, inadequate or improper sealing, and that all the seams are even. Most tanks come with a limited guarantee, so it is important to test your aquarium with water as soon as possible. It's a good idea to use this wastewater to clean the tank, but *do not* use soap or detergents, just water and a soft cloth or towel. If there is sealant residue on the glass, it can be removed with a razor blade. When testing for leaks, be sure the aquarium is on a firm, level surface, preferably the very stand or location on which it will permanently rest.

Outfitting Your New Aquarium

Needless to say, you will find it necessary to purchase a good deal of equipment to set up your tank. While many items might be considered a luxury, others are a necessity. Carefully study the checklist of equipment below, and discuss it with your local pet shop personnel:

- Tank and stand
- Decorations, including background
- Gravel
- Air pump and related items
- Filter (various types)
- Heater and thermometer
- Hood with light
- pH kit, siphon hose
- Food, remedies, and a book on fish diseases
- Extension cord (optional)

These items are essential, and it would be difficult to maintain a "modified" balanced aquarium without them. Let's look at each item and learn what is best for your situation. We have already covered the tank selection adequately. Always place the tank near an electrical outlet. The back of the aquarium should be at least 10 to 12 inches from the wall, so there is room to reach behind it to adjust hanging equipment such as filters, pumps, or gang valves. Whatever the tank sits on must be sufficiently strong to support the weight of the entire setup; a 20-gallon long tank complete with gravel will weigh about 175 pounds—enough said!

After you have tested your tank, select a suitable location, and place the tank on its permanent base.

Background

An essential part of any tank's décor is the background. While it may also be aesthetically pleasing, it serves the useful purpose of providing security for the fishes. There is an endless variety of very colorful and interesting designs from which to choose. You may select a natural setting or a simple, solid color motif. Backgrounds typically are taped to the outside of the tank; some are self-adhesive.

You might consider a background of natural rock (usually shale) or some sort of molded design that hangs in the tank and thus plays an integral role in the tank environment. Many small cichlids (pronounced *sick-lids*) like to hide in the rocky crevices.

Gravel

Next comes the gravel. There is a wide variety from which to choose; you can select the composition, texture, grain size, and color. Natural gravel is preferred by anyone wishing to create an atmosphere as close to the real thing as possible. This is an off-white, stone-colored gravel (usually #1 or #2 in grain size)that is simply crushed rock or natural riverbed stone. If you prefer dark, natural-colored gravel, you might try red flint. It will add a dash of color to the substrate. Mixtures of different gravels also look attractive. The amount of gravel you will require depends on the size of your aquarium and how deep you want the gravel. In general, one

Dark-colored gravel is more likely to show off your fish's colors better compared to light-colored gravel.

Wash Your Gravel

Before adding the gravel to the tank, it must be thoroughly washed in warm tap water to remove all the dirt and unwanted extraneous material. The gravel will need to be thoroughly rinsed until the wastewater is clear. When this occurs, the gravel should be clean and ready to put into the tank. It is a good idea to buy a 2- or 3-gallon plastic bucket strictly for aquarium use. The bucket can be used to remove and replace water in the tank. Never rinse gravel in a bucket that has had detergent in it.

to two pounds per gallon is the correct range. Let's say you are going to employ an undergravel filter and/or maintain a large number of plants. For this you will want your gravel a bit deeper, so the roots will have sufficient room to develop. In this case, two inches is necessary. If, on the other hand, you do not expect to use a large number of plants, you might make the gravel as shallow as one inch.

Pour the clean gravel into the clean tank, and add enough water to just cover the top of the gravel. If you are using an undergravel filter, you must place it in the tank before adding the gravel. Level the gravel so that it is of equal depth in all locations. You may now proceed to fill the tank half full. Be sure to use a chlorine remover or similar water conditioner in the water. Use water in the 80° to 85°F range, since you will be working in it for a while, and there is no sense working in cold water. As you add the water, use your cupped hand or a soup dish to prevent the stream from scattering gravel all about. After you reach a certain water depth, the water itself will act as a cushion if you do not pour from too great a height.

Utilizing Air Pumps

It is now time to utilize a good deal of the equipment you have purchased. This will include (1) the air pump itself, (2) airline (plastic tubing), (3) a gang valve, and (4) a pump hanger (if needed). The air pump is used to introduce air into the aquarium. This may be accomplished through a filter or an airstone. The air is essential to the operation of a successful "modified" balanced aquarium. It creates a current that moves water from the bottom to the top and permits a greater exchange of gases as the air and water interface. In short, the dissolved oxygen content of the water is increased, and the carbon dioxide content is decreased. Since fish extract oxygen from the water in order to breathe, it is important that the CO_2 level be low because a high level of CO_2 inhibits fish respiration.

You must select your air pump based on the number of air supply outlets you need. More powerful pumps cost more money. For the average 20- or 30-gallon community tank, three outlets are usually sufficient. Place your pump hanger on the back of the aquarium, and set the pump on it. Run a piece of airline tubing from the pump to the gang valve. Now, connect each filter, airstone, or other air-operated device to a piece of airline tubing, and attach the pieces of airline tubing to the gang valve. Plug in the pump, and adjust all outlets to a reasonable level. It is important that the pump be locat-

The bubbles created by using an airpump are not only pleasing to the eye but also allow the fishes to breathe easier.

Plastic plants are popular with hobbyists who do not want to keep live plants.

ed above the water's surface, for if it is below there is a possibility that water could siphon into the pump if the power fails. Even if you intend to use a power filter instead of an inside filter, you can still employ an airstone to circulate the water better.

Aquarium Decorations

The next step is to put in the decorations and plants you have purchased. If you have decided on the natural approach, you will be using driftwood, rocks, and live plants. These should all be rinsed in tap water and the plants disinfected. Your pet shop will help you select the necessary disinfectant solution, usually potassium permanganate. If you are constructing caves with rocks, be sure they are stable and will not collapse if any fishes start to dig the gravel out from under them.

Take a final look at your completed décor, and be sure you are satisfied with it. Add the rest of the water until the tank is almost full. It is quite likely that you have already placed a filter in the tank if you are using an undergravel filter. If you have decided on an inside filter or a power filter to hang on the back of the aquarium, now is the time to set it up. In a 20- or 30-gallon tank, an undergravel filter and a mechanical filter

Artificial driftwood will not alter the pH or hardness of your water like real driftwood does.

work well in conjunction. A single power filter with two airstones in the tank will work equally well. Obvious constituents of any corner filter include filter floss and activated carbon. If you have already plugged in the air pump and the power filter, you will have probably recognized the need for an extension cord.

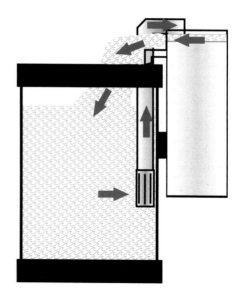

Filtration

There are two popular types of power filters

Filtration Diagram: the red arrows indicate dirty water while the blue arrows indicate clean, filtered water.

available today. One draws water from the tank through siphon tubes; the water flows through the filter material and is pumped back into the tank via an output tube. The other filters are called overflow models. They draw water in by a single tube and then push it through the filter material. It returns by cascading like a waterfall into the tank. Both work well.

There are many other filtering schemes as well. Canister filters are high volume and not recommended for small tanks. Trickle filters and many varieties of biological filtration are too messy and too delicate for beginners. But as you gather experience and more tanks, your appreciation of more advanced filtration techniques will be enhanced.

Heaters

Everything, it is hoped, has gone well up until now. If so, you should place the heater in the aquarium (but not plugged in yet),

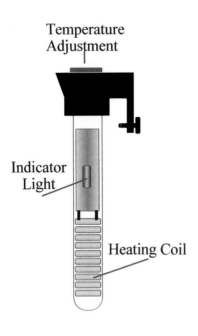

Temperature Adjustment

Indicator Light

Heating Coil

Heaters are an important piece of equipment for any tropical fish tank.

and allow 60 minutes for it to reach the same temperature as the water. There are two basic types of heaters: One remains completely submerged while the other, partially submerged, attaches to the side of the aquarium. Both work well, but the submerged type can be hidden better. Select the appropriate size heater by using the formula of five watts per gallon. Thus, a 20-gallon tank requires a 100-watt heater, and a 30-gallon requires 150 watts. Plug the heater in and turn the dial just until the pilot light comes on. Check the temperature with a thermometer that has been tested for accuracy. If the temperature is too low, simply turn the knob a notch or two (in the proper direction), and wait for the pilot light to go off. If the aquarium is warmer than the usual 78° to 82°F, you must wait for it to cool down before you set the thermostat, which is built into the heater.

Covers & Canopies

Aside from the fishes, the final touch is the hood, which should completely cover the tank. Along the back a strip of flexible plastic is normally provided, so cut-outs can be made to fit the equipment being used. A lamp, preferably fluorescent, will be situated in the middle, with a hinged flap in front to provide access to the tank. Your pet shop or aquarium store salesperson should show you how to set up all the accessories you buy.

Selecting Fishes

The time has finally arrived to purchase fishes for your aquarium. Your tank should be set up for *at least* 96 hours before you begin to add fishes. Be sure the water is perfectly clear and all filters and pumps are working properly. The water temperature should be in the 78° to 82°F range. Check to see if the pH is between 6.8 and 7.2. If all factors are "go" you may proceed. To some extent this is the easiest part of the entire tank setup operation. It is certainly the most exciting. You might merely select the fish you like rather than opting for specific types. Such haphazard selections usually result in problems, but few community tanks are totally problem free. You must be ready to accept the fact that not every fish you buy will prove to be a suitable resident. Some will be too aggressive, others too timid.

On the whole, however, relatively few problems will occur if you follow the suggestions of a knowledgeable pet dealer or check in the *Atlas of Freshwater Aquarium Fishes* to determine the temperament and eventual size of the fishes which interest you.

Certain types of fishes are better for the community tank than others. The distinction may be due to size, breeding habits, feeding requirements, or temperament. For instance, if you know a certain fish will outgrow its tankmates and maybe even its tank, it would not be a good choice. Some fishes become very territorial and aggressive when they breed, and these may destroy not only other fishes but the aquarium décor as well. Predatory fishes might eat their tankmates and are, therefore, not recommended. Other fishes are very timid and prefer to hide a great deal; they could easily starve to death in a community tank. An extremely interesting, colorful, and varied assortment of fishes can be selected from a few groups of fishes. Each group has the distinction of being relatively easy to maintain; they accept a wide range of water conditions and eat almost anything. Also, these fishes are comparatively non-aggressive and relatively inexpensive. Let's meet them now.

Platys come in many colors and are very popular with beginning hobbyists.

Livebearers

Livebearers are probably the most popular fishes for beginners. They give birth to free-swimming young that are miniature reproductions of the female when they are born. These fry (fish babies) are relatively large for newborn fish, and they are perfectly capable of taking care of themselves as long as their parents or other fishes in the tank do not eat them. When a female livebearer

Swordtails also come in many colors and usually grow slightly larger than their close cousins—the platys.

is noticeably heavy with young, she should be placed in a breeding trap where the young can be protected after they are born. There is no trick at all to breeding livebearers except that a male and female are necessary. These are easily distinguished since the male of the species has his anal fin modified into a breeding organ known as the *gonopodium*. The female's anal fin is typically wedge shaped. One of the outstanding aspects of keeping livebearers is that you will find a huge array of different fishes available. There are actually only a handful of species involved, but they have been developed into a multitude of varieties by fish farms around the world. As it turns out, the genetic makeup of many livebearers is quite plastic, and new strains can be created in only a few generations.

Most livebearers are capable of reproducing between three and four months of age, so several generations can be produced each year. The most common livebearers include guppies, platys, swordtails, and mollies. *Poecilia reticulata* (guppy) is considered the king of all genetic-bred species, for it is available in numerous colors with different fin shapes. Unfortunately, guppies do not make the very best community fish since the males are quite small and have very long, flowing fins that might be nipped by other fishes. This does not mean they cannot be kept, but that care must be taken in selecting their tankmates.

Selecting Fishes

Mollies prefer to have some salt added to their water.

Perhaps better choices are the platys (*Xiphophorus maculatus* and *Xiphophorus variatus*) and swordtails (*Xiphophorus helleri*) that are closely related fishes and every bit as desirable as the guppy. They reach 2.5 to 4 inches in length and can defend themselves. Mollies (*Poecilia latipinna, P. velifera*, and *P. sphenops*) are very popular, but they prefer some salt added to their water and a diet high in vegetable matter. Also, they may grow quite large, and this could cause problems later on. Really, the choice is yours, and there is no good reason to

Schooling Fishes

When buying fishes that are known to form schools, it is essential that you purchase six to eight individuals, or they will not exhibit their schooling behavior. The major types of fishes to consider within this grouping are tetras, barbs, rasboras, danios, and rainbows. Many of the species in these groups remain small enough at maximum size to comfortably fit in the community tank.

reject any of these fishes, for their shortcomings are negligible. Again, you are referred to the *Atlas of Freshwater Fishes* where 9,000 color photos and short, descriptive captions make selections simple.

Schooling Fishes

This is an artificial grouping which contains many different types of fishes, but all of them tend to swim in schools if their numbers are sufficient. Most of these fishes reproduce by scattering eggs, so they might alternatively be known as *egglayers*. It would be relatively unusual to spawn any of these species in the aquarium and have their fry survive, but the purpose of a balanced community tank is to observe the fish, not to have them reproduce. (That can come later if you decide to specialize with a specific group of fishes.)

Tetras

Tetras are found in South and Central America, as well as Africa. They are generally small, colorful fishes that live in schools and are found in quiet, slow-moving waters. Except for a bit of fin nipping, most small tetras can be kept without difficulty. You might wish to select a few species from the following recommended list to include in your community aquarium:

Hemigrammus caudovittatus, **Buenos Aires Tetra**

H. erythrozonus, **Glowlight Tetra**

H. ocellifer, **Head & Tail light Tetra**

Petitella georgiae, **Rummy-nose Tetra**

Hyphessobrycon flammeus, **Flame Tetra**

H. erythrostigma, **Bleeding Heart Tetra**

H. herbertaxelrodi, **Black Neon Tetra**

H. serpae, **Serpae Tetra**

Paracheirodon axelrodi, **Cardinal Tetra**

Gymnocorymbus ternetzi, **Black Tetra**

Paracheirodon innesi, **Neon Tetra**

Lemon Tetras are an easy-to-care-for schooling species.

Barbs

Barbs tend to be a bit more aggressive than tetras, and they frequently grow larger, too. They are mostly found in Asia and Africa, but the majority of the species in the hobby come from Asia. Color varieties and long-finned strains of barbs and danios have been developed. Some of the species available include:

Puntius everetti, Clown Barb

P. lateristriga, T-barb

P. semifasciolatus, Half-striped Barb

P. oligolepis, Checker Barb

P. titteya, Cherry Barb

P. tetrazona, Tiger Barb

P. conchonius, Rosy Barb

P. filamentosus, Black-spot Barb

P. lineatus, Striped Barb

P. nigrofasciatus, Black Ruby Barb

P. ticto, Tic-Tac-Toe Barb

A smaller number of barbs are necessary to form a school than with tetras, and since they are aggressive feeders, too many might eat more than their fair share. Of all the schooling fishes mentioned

The Green Tiger Barb is a color variant of the ever-popular Tiger Barb.

here, barbs are the worst fin nippers. This does not mean they should be left out of the community tank; instead, they should be used sparingly, not in large numbers.

Rasboras

Rasboras and danios are cyprinids that are closely related. The major difference is that danios have barbels while rasboras do not. There is hardly a species of either which cannot be kept in the community tank. Schools of six to ten fish are graceful and active and mix well with all fishes. Danios swim mostly at the surface while rasboras inhabit the upper to middle regions of the tank. Some small and peaceful cyprinid species to look for include:

Brachydanio albolineatus, Pearl Danio

B. rerio, Zebra Danio

Rasbora borapotensis, Red-tailed Rasbora

R. einthoveni, Brilliant Rasbora

R. kalochroma, Big-spot Rasbora

R. trilineatus, Scissortail Rasbora

Tanichthys albonubes, White Cloud Mountain Minnow

T. micagemmae, Black-line White Cloud

Trigonostigma heteromorpha, Harlequin Rasbora

Although a school of beautiful fishes can be a spectacular sight, it is probably unwise to mix too many species of schooling fishes together. Experimentation is the key to the right combination. The final group of schooling fishes you can add to your tank is known as rainbows. They are in the families Melanotaeniidae and Atherinidae, and their range is mainly restricted to New Guinea and Australia. They are different from most other fishes in that they have two dorsal fins and are reminiscent to some degree of minnows in the way they behave. Like *Rasbora*, rainbows can be said to be totally innocuous, and they will rarely harm, chase, or harass other fishes. A number of species are available, and as the name implies, rainbows are extremely colorful fishes that deserve a spot in any community aquarium.

Harlequin Rasboras are generally peaceful and do well in a small school.

Cichlids

The family Cichlidae contains over 1,500 species, and many of these are popular aquarium fishes. Unfortun-ately, a large number of them grow too large, are too aggressive, or dig up the gravel too much to be considered good community tank inhabitants. A group of Neotropical species, however, grows no larger than four inches and rarely digs or attacks their tankmates. These are commonly known as dwarf cichlids and include such species as:

Mikrogeophagus ramirezi, **Ram (Gold Ram)**
Apistogramma agassizi, **Spade-tailed Dwarf Cichlid**
A. borelli, **Borelli's Dwarf Cichlid**
Nannacara anomala, **Golden Dwarf Cichlid**
Crenicara filamentosa, **Checkerboard Cichlid**

Freshwater Angelfish are probably the most popular species of cichlid.

A few larger cichlids are peaceful and do well in the community situation. These include the *Heros severum* (gold and regular types), *Mesonauta festivum* (Flag Cichlid), and *Pterophyllum* (Angelfishes) species. Angels have been bred into a number of strains such as silver (wild), marble, blushing, half-black, black, zebra, and gold.

A Hint About Cichlids

Cichlids tend to be territorial to a great extent, and this means they may try to defend a specific object in the tank, such as a rock or a piece of driftwood. If you have too many cichlids, it won't be long before they have the tank divided into a series of battle zones. Obviously, you must restrict the number of cichlids so that other fishes in the tank will be able to go about their business unhindered. It is best, therefore, to select no more than two specimens of any cichlid species.

Many of the mouthbrooding cichlids from Africa, especially the riverine *Haplochromis*, may be kept if you are prepared for a good deal of digging activity. It is quite possible to breed mouthbrooders in a community tank and retrieve the fry. They frequently escape from their parents' mouths to prosper and grow up in the tank. The cichlids of the Rift Lakes of Africa are considered too rough for normal community tanks, and they also require water conditions (very hard and alkaline), most community fish would do poorly in—but they *can* be kept in communities of their own kind.

Finally, if you don't mind a bit of gravel rearrangement, the *Geophagus* and *Satanoperca* species from South America are relatively peaceful, even though they grow to a fairly large size. A community tank without cichlids is like a cake without icing. These highly evolved fishes exhibit interesting and diverse behavior traits.

Bottom Dwellers

The next group of fishes recommended for every community tank is the bottom-dwellers, often wrongly thought of as scavengers. These are primarily catfishes, spiny eels, loaches, algae-eaters, and some species of "sharks" (cyprinids in the genus

Cory catfishes should be kept in small groups, so they feel comfortable.

Red-tailed Sharks are excellent additions to a community tank.

Epalzeorhynchos). Catfish in the genus *Corydoras* are familiar aquarium residents and are totally peaceful. There are over 100 species of *Corydoras*, and many are available in your local pet shop. Other acceptable catfishes include the smaller of the suckermouth species in the family Loricariidae. Many catfishes grow too large for a community tank, so check with your dealer on which ones are suitable.

Loaches come in a variety of shapes and sizes, and all the kuhlii loaches will add a touch of excitement to your tank. Likewise, some spiny eels are comical and harmless alternatives to the loaches. Be careful, however, for some eels grow too large for a community tank.

The red-tailed shark (*Epalzeorhynchos bicolor*) and the red-finned shark (*E. erythurus*) make interesting additions to the community tank. They are constantly on the move, searching every crevice for something to eat. Unfortunately, they often enjoy chasing other fishes around the tank. This sort of behavior gets out of hand sometimes, especially if there are two sharks. Limit your shark selection to a single fish.

Selecting Fishes

It is obvious that a tank can support only a limited number of bottom-dwellers, so you will have to be selective and choose only those fishes that really appeal to you. Probably four bottom-dwellers are enough for a 20- to 30-gallon tank.

Anabantoids

These species are commonly known as bubble-nest builders or labyrinth fishes. They possess an accessory breathing organ that permits them to extract oxygen from the air. The use of this organ is so vital that fishes trapped below the surface will die, since their gills cannot extract enough oxygen from the water alone. There are three types of anabantoids to consider (1) paradise fishes, (2) bettas, and (3) gouramis. Paradise fishes were one of the first types of tropical fishes kept in the home aquarium. They actually prefer relatively cool waters since they are found primarily in China, but they do well even at temperatures up to 84°F. There is only one species of paradise fish readily available; it can be found in an albino form. *Macropodus opercularis* is the common paradise fish. Only a single pair of these fish should be kept in a community tank.

Dwarf Gouramis are beautiful and stay relatively small compared to many other gouramis.

A community of mixed Gouramis is sure to please the eye.

Betta splendens, better known as the Siamese fighting fish, is one of the most popular aquarium fishes. Unfortunately, males tend to be very aggressive and cannot be kept together even in a large community tank. One male may be kept along with several females, but you might expect the females to show some wear and tear due to the male's chasing. One of the major drawbacks to *Betta splendens* is the same one that applies to the guppy. Males of both species have long, flowing fins, and these tend to be nipped, ripped, or torn by various fishes in the tank. There are several other species of *Betta* in the aquarium hobby, and any one of these would be a good choice for the community environment. Once again, only a single male should be kept per tank.

Gouramis are extremely popular aquarium fishes, and there are quite a few species available to the hobbyist. Virtually any of these are satisfactory for the community aquarium, but some grow considerably larger than others. Gouramis in the genus *Colisa* tend to be small, never reaching more than three inches in length, while gouramis in the genus *Trichogaster* may reach ten inches, but more normally grow to only six inches. Fish in either genus are acceptable, although *Colisa* gouramis tend to be less

Selecting Fishes

Bettas come in many different colors and patterns. This one is showing a lot of purple.

aggressive, and more of them can be kept together. Some of the fishes you might wish to purchase include:

> *Colisa lalia*, Dwarf Gourami
>
> *C. chuna*, Honey Gourami
>
> *C. labiosus*, Thick-lipped Gourami
>
> *Trichogaster trichopterus*, Blue Gourami
>
> *T. leeri*, Pearl Gourami
>
> *T. microlepis*, Moonlight Gourami

The blue (three-spot) gourami has been developed into several different varieties including the Cosby (marbled gourami), the gold, and the platinum gourami. Recently developed strains of the small species include the fire gourami and the golden honey gourami. If you decide to keep *Colisa* gouramis in your tank, you may keep more than a single pair of any species or you may keep several species together. With the *Trichogaster* types, it is advisable to have only a pair or trio of any one species per tank.

If you have decided to keep very small fishes in your community tank, there is another species of gourami that reaches only

1.5inches in length. This is the sparkling (pygmy) gourami, *Trichopsis pumilus*. It does very well when housed with smaller, non-aggressive fishes. Do not try to keep it with any of the larger gouramis in the genera *Colisa* and *Trichogaster*.

Since gouramis are anabantoids, they will spend a certain portion of their time going to the surface and gulping air. When keeping labyrinth fishes in the community tank, you must be careful that the water's surface is not choked with plants. This might prevent the fish from obtaining sufficient air. Also, there is the kissing gourami, *Helostoma temmincki*. Though interesting, it grows too large for the small tank.

Goldfish & Koi

Many aquarists do not consider goldfish or koi as aquarium fishes. This should not be. There are many exotic, bizarre, and even grotesque forms

Red Cap Orandas are one of the most sought-after strains of fancy goldfish.

of goldfish and koi that must be maintained in the aquarium, since they could not survive in the typical garden pool environment.

Besides adding color, goldfish and koi are peaceful, hardy, relatively inexpensive, and interesting. The small ones are especially ideal for the community tank.

Ask your pet shop dealer to show you some of the various fancy goldfish and koi varieties, some of which make great additions to the community aquarium. Feeding them is easy, too. They eat everything that you normally offer your other community tank fishes, whether it be live, frozen, freeze-dried, or the more usual flake foods. They also do a lot of scavenging in the aquarium gravel.

Foods & Feeding

Foods suitable for aquarium fishes come in various forms. Many of them have been formulated into prepared feeds that are offered for sale through pet retailers and local aquarium shops. These prepared feeds are probably the best way for beginning hobbyists to provide a broad range of nutrients to their fishes, but there are also many other ways to do this, and that is really what this chapter is all about.

The first thing hobbyists seeking knowledge about feeding fish should do, whether experienced or not, is to familiarize themselves with the various forms of fish foods that are available. It is surprising how many foods are suitable, and often of quite good quality, but are rarely used due to a lack of information on them. Another issue that concerns hobbyists is the lack of availability of many foods. This is especially true with the various live foods.

Live Foods

In most cases, offering live foods to your fishes is the best way to supply them with a broad range of useful nutrients and vitamins. However, live foods can also be the highway for transmittable diseases, so proper precautions should always be taken to ensure that they are fresh and disease free before offering them to your fishes. When possible, the source of these foods should be known to make certain that they are coming from disease-free sources. This is especially important with live *Tubifex* and blackworms, since they are probably the best-known live foods to regularly harbor pathogens.

Tubifex and Blackworms

While tubifex worms (*Tubifex, Limnodrilus,* and other lesser known genera) and blackworms (*Lumbriculus variegatus*) are completely different animals from a taxonomic viewpoint, they are very similar regarding their care, culture, and feeding to aquarium fishes.

Blackworms should be clean and healthy looking before being offered to your fishes.

Keep Your Worms Fresh!

Both tubifex worms and blackworms are best if purchased fresh and as needed. Whether that be daily, weekly, or monthly, they can go sour very fast and need to be kept very cool and in very clean water in order to survive even a few hours. Pet shops usually have their stocks replenished twice weekly and are set up to handle these organisms, so it really is best to buy them as you need them.

Additionally, it should be noted that "tubifex" is a catch-all name for many organisms that are all closely related. In Asia, most high profile Discus breeders offer heavy feedings of tubifex worms. They do this mainly to provide their broodstock with an easy-to-use, easy-to-culture food that is exceedingly high in protein and nutrients.

Years ago, Pierre Brichard—a world famous exporter of cichlids from Lake Tanganyika—would culture tubifex worms for use as fish food to offer the fishes awaiting export to the United States and Europe. He would offer them to the fishes in large balls once or twice daily. Brichard believed that there was no other food that could repair the damage that a fish experienced from capture the way tubifex worms could. Of course, he used a good food source, good water (from the lake itself), and expensive medications to accomplish this, but he always came back and gave the majority of the credit to the worms.

The proper care and handling of even a small amount of tubifex worms and blackworms is *extremely* important. It is not uncommon to hear of hobbyists who purchased these worms and then stopped off at the grocery store to pick up dinner and at the movie rental place to pick up some entertainment, and by the time they arrived home their worms were a sloppy gray mess. Such a scenario may seem humorous, but it is far too common. What is even

Foods & Feeding

more shocking is the number of hobbyists who don't think anything of it and dump the entire contents of the container in their aquariums!

The almost instantaneous result is usually a very cloudy, smelly aquarium. You will know it is bad when your fishes, that usually come over to eat the worms very greedily, make a 180° turn and swim frantically to get away from the slimy gray blob that just invaded their beloved home. To combat such a situation, you will need to perform several massive water changes, and you will absolutely need to test very often for heightened levels of ammonia and nitrite. Such water changes in and of themselves can upset your aquarium in a major way, but when combined with such pollution—watch out!

Hopefully, the seriousness of keeping these worms clean is very clear. Now, we can focus on the good side of using these as an effective food source.

The addition of these worms to a regular feeding regimen is highly suggested for several reasons. First and foremost, feeding them to your fishes will offer raw animal protein in a way that they are likely to recognize immediately as food and consume with gusto. Second, the range of nutrients that these organisms offer is completely different than that offered by most other foods—not necessarily better, but certainly different. To a lesser extent, by feeding live worms to your fishes, especially those maintained in a fully setup aquarium, you offer them a unique opportunity to hunt and seek out prey as if they were in nature. This is probably more beneficial to their psyche than anything else, and that is great—fish deserve to have fun, too!

When it comes time to actually feeding the worms to your fishes, you should do so in a way that allows the fish maximum access to them. The use of a worm feeder is a very effective method of accom-

Worm feeders are recommended for feeding all types of live worms, except Eearthworms.

plishing this. Worm feeders generally have holes that are the proper size to allow the tubifex or blackworms easy passage through them. Most units commercially available through your local pet shop will have some type of attachment on them that will allow you to affix the unit to the side of the aquarium. Others may have a hollow ring around the top that holds air and allows the feeder to float freely on the water's surface.

The amount of worms that are offered to your fishes at any one time should be carefully calculated. You should not place such a large amount in the feeder that many   free-fall to the gravel surface. Aquariums that have bare bottoms are not included in this discussion, because bare-bottomed tanks can easily be siphoned of excess worms, and the worms can be recycled for use in another feeding. Blackworms are known for their ability to invade the aquarium's gravel and live for many months. They will often reproduce, and some advanced hobbyists have actually used them effectively to remove excess detritus in show tanks.

Foods & Feeding

Another Worm Hint

One other important note about feeding fishes with tubifex and blackworms is the high-nutrient content of the waste. Fishes fed a steady diet high in animal matter will have waste that is very nutrient-rich. Such nutrient-rich waste fouls the water very quickly and can cause major water quality issues.

Only allow the fishes to feast on these until they have rounded off bellies, or in other words, until they reach their satiation point. You may be quite surprised to learn just how many worms it takes for a small tetra to reach satiation, let alone an entire school of them. You can go through a golf ball-sized amount of worms in no time if feeding a lot of smaller fish or just a few bigger ones.

If you feel that you have overfed your fishes or may have fed them spoiled worms, the best thing to do is conduct a series of small water changes, and test for ammonia and nitrite hourly for about eight hours. The following day, you should test at least four times during the day or until you feel that the threat has subsided. If in fact you did feed your fish spoiled worms and your aquarium is starting to smell turn cloudy, you should do a series of large water changes and follow the same guidelines for testing as above. Always be sure to add water that has either been aged or conditioned with a tap-water conditioner. As with most supplies, a good conditioner should be available at your local fish shop.

Fresh Foods

Fresh foods are generally defined as any foods that are not living, have not been frozen, and have not been processed in any way other than field dressing or cleaning. Fresh foods are perhaps the best types of food available to hobbyists today. In nearly every case, freshly collected foods offer all of the pros of live foods with hardly any of the cons.

Frozen Foods

Many of the foods listed above are also available in frozen form. Generally, frozen foods have the same overall nutritional value as live or fresh foods, but they are easier to store since you can keep them in your freezer. However, the longer they are frozen, the less nutritional they become. This is primarily due to the crystalline structure of ice and the damage the ice does to the cells of the food.

Frozen foods are only good for so long. Usually, it is recommended that you keep a package of frozen food no longer than one month

Helpful Hints to Feeding Frozen Foods

Feeding frozen foods is highly recommended due to their diversity and freshness. Most frozen foods are easily broken into smaller pieces and can be stored and thawed in individual packages so as to not expose the whole lot to air on a daily basis. They have to be fed in a way that is safe for your fishes.

To feed a piece of frozen food to your fish, simply place the piece to be fed in a small volume of water taken directly from the aquarium. Next, allow the food to thaw completely, stirring gently to not break up the food too much. Thawing usually takes 15 minutes or so. Then, gently strain all of the water out of the thawing container by pouring the contents of the container through an appropriately sized net or actually removing the food by hand. In the case of larger foods like whole fish or shrimp, rinse the foods in clean tank water before offering them. Formulations should be added slowly to prevent overfeeding, as should smaller foods like Mysid Shrimp and Brine Shrimp. Only feed as much as your fish will actively consume and not let hit the bottom of the aquarium. Feed frozen foods often, but when possible, alternate them with a high-quality prepared food.

before replacing it with a fresher package—but even a month is stretching it. Frozen foods exposed to air at least twice weekly (from pulling out the package to break off a piece of food), will begin to show signs of "dry rot." This is the condition where the very cold dry air in the freezer dries out the frozen food to the point that it becomes useless.

Freeze-dried Foods

Some organisms are best stored when they go through a process known as lyophilization, or freeze-drying. These organisms are preserved whole, in their original configuration, and with nearly all of their essential nutrients intact. However, such foods can be expensive compared with their frozen counterparts. Nearly all foods offered as freeze-dried are also offered as live, fresh, and frozen, so you do have options.

One species that is not offered as live, somewhat regularly offered as frozen, and very commonly offered as freeze-dried is Krill. Krill are

Some types of freeze-dried foods can actually be pressed against the glass for the fish to pick at.

small, shrimp-like creatures that inhabit the cold subarctic waters of both the northern and southern hemispheres. They are rich in nutrients and provide outstanding color-enhancing characteristics with their potent alpha- and beta-carotenes.

Feeding a wide variety of foods to your fishes is always the best choice. If you have freezers available, perhaps you should opt to use more of the frozen foods, but if not, don't be discouraged. As with most things, each type of food has its loyal supporters, but in the end, variety is the key.

Prepared Foods

Nearly all of the foods available to modern hobbyists are prepared in some way or another. In actuality, even frozen and freeze-dried foods are prepared foods, but we treat them differently due to the vastness of this category. Instead, we will cover several types of foods that are traditionally considered to be prepared. Such foods are flaked foods, pelleted foods, wafers, and liquid foods.

Flaked Foods

There is perhaps no other type of fish food that comes close to flaked (or flake) foods in terms of numbers of containers produced and sold. Flake foods have been around for decades. Many brands and formulations have come and gone, with some being better in quality than others.

Flake foods are the most popular food available to hobbyists, both fresh and marine. They come in an assortment of colors, compositions, textures, and sizes. In fact, a can of flake food is often one of the first things a new hobbyist picks up.

Although flaked food is readily available, is it necessarily the best choice of food to feed your fishes? Flake foods are not bad, and many are in fact very good. However, they should be fed with the same discretion as freeze-dried and prepared foods.

These juvenile Discus have very small mouths and need small food particles in order to eat normally.

In addition to being of higher quality, another thing that flake foods have going for them is their diversity. There are flake foods formulated out of just about everything.

Little fishes usually have little mouths and need smaller foods to feed on. Unfortunately, most insects are too big for fishes such as tetras, barbs, danios, and rasboras, but flake foods that are formulated with insects are the perfect size for their tiny mouths. Only with a prepared food can we add such things as earthworms, tubifex worms, and crickets to our feeding regimen.

Such foods are not often found, but when they are, they should be purchased, because insects are an outstanding source of natural vitamins and minerals for fishes. Just as some frozen foods fall under the unique category, we have some flake foods that deserve the same treatment. If it can be added to a paste, it can become an ingredient in flake foods. Some unique flaked foods include (with their targeted benefits):

• Earthworms (unique nutrients)

• Tubifex Worms (unique nutrients)

• Crickets (insect nutrients)

• Bee Pollen (color enhancement)

- *Spirulina* Powder (color and vigor enhancement)
- Beef heart (weight-gaining properties)
- Chicken (unique nutrients)
- Liver (iron)
- Bone Meal (extra calcium)
- Bananas (potassium)
- Blood Meal (color enhancement /appetite stimulant)
- Krill Meal (color enhancement)
- Marine Sponges (unique range of vitamins)
- Marine Algae (color enhancement)

As you can see, the list is quite long, and this just barely scratches the surface of what hobbyists and professionals alike have produced. As with all foods, variation is the key, and it is strongly recommended that you vary the diet of your fishes as often as possible. The next time you are at your local fish shop, check out the ingredients of several flake foods before you buy just one.

Clown Loaches do well with prepared foods in pellet or wafer form.

Pelleted Foods and Wafers

Like flake foods, pelleted foods are available in a huge assortment of colors, compositions, textures, and sizes. However, unlike flake foods, pellets seem to hold their nutritional value longer, so the fish ingests a more nutrient-packed piece of food.

Pellets can be harmful in aquariums with brisk water movement. Just like flakes, pellets have a tendency to find every possible spot to fall into and begin decaying. Watch out for this when feeding, and only feed a few at a time. After they have been consumed, add a few more. If you have very aggressive fishes, perhaps a few automatic feeders set to go off at the same time will suit you better. After all, no fish can be in two places at once. Placing one at each end of the aquarium is the best alternative in this situation. For very large aquariums (more than 8 feet in length), three or even four automatic feeders are recommended.

One very nasty trait of pellets is that they expand after ingestion. Flakes do this, too, but to a much lesser extent. Being dry, or nearly dry, pellets take in water and expand. The same happens to a piece of dog food kibble that falls into the dog's water bowl. Fish do not compensate for this expansion right away, and it can cause them great distress. So, you must take such a potential problem into account. This is more reason not to overfeed your fishes!

Wafers are flattened pellets that are usually formulated for bottom-feeders, since they most often sink. There are several types on the market. One type is made out of a vegetarian-based formula and intended to provide herbivores with a quick and easy meal after the lights go out, and the others are designed for carnivorous fishes. All types are offered in multiple sizes and a few shapes. The majority are flattened, pancake-like disks, but there are also star-shaped pellets. They all serve the same purpose and add a little more variety to a fish's diet.

General Feeding Concepts

A concept is an abstract or generic idea that has been generalized from a particular experience or instance. The feeding concepts mentioned here will likely differ from the concepts of others, just as they individually differ based on our own unique experiences.

By now, you should have a good grasp of what foods to use in what quantities and when to feed them. Feeding your fishes is a rewarding experience. It is something that families should participate in together. Whether it is once or three times a day, young people should be included, because it is something that is educational and takes time to learn how to do properly. It is a science as well as an art.

Generally, fishes should be fed daily. However, such a generalization is marked with controversy right from the start and needs to be made more specific. So, what if we said that community fishes need to be fed daily, but predatory fishes need to be fed three times weekly? This is a little better, but what if we have a community of predatory fishes?

The Right Food at the Right Time

The fishes' opportunity to eat depends largely on you, the hobbyist, and when you are going to offer them food. More often than not, they will eat—or try to eat—whatever you put in front of them. This can be good and bad. It's especially bad when you make a conscious decision to feed them the wrong foods. It can be good when you make a similar decision and offer them the right foods in the right amounts at the right times.

To further complicate matters, what about opportunistic predatory fishes or fishes that would not consume another animal unless it was there for the taking? Are tetras predatory? Not in the general sense, but they do prey on water fleas.

What we are implying here is that all fish are basically predatory in one sense or another. This is an important concept to learn and understand. The feeding of fishes has more to do with opportunity and metabolism than anything else.

Let's break this down a little further to provide as much clarification as possible. Remember, these are guidelines for feeding your fishes, not laws. Your results may be different, and you will need to compensate on many levels, including the temperature you keep your aquarium at, the size of the container or aquarium you have, the stocking density or overall biomass of the aquarium, and the types of fishes you are maintaining.

Communities of Fishes

Aquariums containing community fishes are probably the most popular of all aquariums in households today, but what defines a community? There are communities of peaceful fishes, there are communities of semi-aggressive fishes, and there are communities of aggressive fishes. The proper feeding techniques vary widely with regards to the kind of fish you are keeping.

Predatory Fishes

Predatory fishes often get special care in the sense that they are treated differently than those species that happily eat flaked foods and pellets with a dash of frozen foods once in a while. They are often thought of as being more sensitive and finicky species. The truth is they are generally quite easy to keep.

A community of small, peaceful fishes should be fed foods that are small in size.

Community Aquariums with Peaceful Fishes

When we think of peaceful fishes, we think of those that are generally harmless to one another or those that are simply not interested in territorial battles or fierce competition over food. While a school of tetras may be predatory against a swarm of *Daphnia*, they are not necessarily considered aggressive. As you will see, we can have many species that are predatory but not technically considered to be aggressive.

Most community aquariums contain an assortment of tetras, barbs, rasboras, or other small, peaceful fishes. Therefore, they need to be fed foods that are rather small in size. Most of the suitable foods for these fishes are either frozen formulas or flakes. Along with these, frozen or live *Daphnia* can be offered in moderate quantities.

Recommended frequency of feeding is highly variable. Fishes in densely stocked aquariums need to be fed at least once per day, but be

These Electric Blue cichlids should be offered a variety of meaty foods.

very careful not to overload the aquarium with too much food. Also keep in mind that more food equals more waste, and more fishes means more food, which equals even more waste. As you can see, such a situation can be very tricky to navigate properly. In the end, it is better to offer less food and keep fewer fish in one aquarium.

Community Aquariums with Predatory Fishes

Just because you have a community aquarium does not mean you have to have peaceful fishes. Many large predatory fishes seem to almost have an unspoken truce between them. It seems as though they know how much damage they are capable of inflicting on each other. Small predatory fishes are very similar in terms of this type of behavior.

Whether you have a community aquarium full of small or large predatory fishes, you will need to offer food in much the same way. Feeding predatory fish is one of the thrills of the aquarium hobby. It is something that is both awesome and scary at the same time. This is especially true with larger predatory fishes, since their food is usually a lot larger. To see a full-grown snakehead strike a large feeder fish is something that nightmares are made of. Often, such a scene is the turning point or the point of no return for those hobbyists wishing to expand their horizons from the average everyday species. Many hard-core predator keepers can still remember the day they converted to the "dark side" of fishkeeping.

In general, predatory fishes need to be fed at least three times per week. The young of most of the bigger species feed on insects and insect larvae, with a transition to larger foods as they grow. Smaller predatory fishes will consume foods that are relatively consistent in size throughout their lives.

The specifics of feeding predatory fishes should be decided on a case-by-case basis, but they all consume meaty foods that are high in protein and nutrients. With this diet comes an increase in the nutrients of the fishes' waste. Therefore, special attention should always be paid to the water chemistry and overall quality. Always be sure to check the ammonia and other nitrogenous compounds in the aquarium's water, and take proactive steps to avoid potential problems.

A species-specific aquarium is just that, a tank with only one species represented.

Foods & Feeding

Species-specific Aquariums

Some hobbyists will set up aquariums with only one species of fish. Sometimes they are predatory, and other times they are not. Regardless, these aquariums are usually the best in terms of ease of feeding for several reasons.

First, since all of the fishes are the same species, they can be offered all the same foods at the same times. Second, with rare exceptions, all of the fish will have similar temperaments and share the same idiosyncrasies. This will allow them to understand each other better and hopefully lessen the risk of severe intraspecific aggression. Third, the fish should have similar growth rates. If one or more fish are not getting their fair share, it will be easy to recognize this and solve the problem before it gets out of hand.

Overall, fishkeepers should heavily research all fish foods before choosing a diet for their fishes. As a responsible hobbyist, you will need to provide a healthy and diverse diet so your fishes will grow and thrive in captivity. There are multiple foods ranging from live microorganisms to freeze-dried shrimps to flaked foods containing earthworms. Use as much of a variety as possible, and you will enjoy many years of happiness with your fishes.

Tank
Maintenance

When you are beginning to fill your aquarium up with fishes, it is important to consider the number of fishes you should keep in your tank. An old rule of thumb goes: an inch of fish (tail excluded) per gallon of water, but this rule can be broken with today's modern filtration and aeration. Even so, if a tank looks overcrowded, you can be sure that it is.

If you have purchased too many fishes, be aware that problems will develop. The fishes will either reduce their numbers through aggression, or environmental conditions will deteriorate to the point that your fishes become diseased. If you wish to maintain even a moderately populated aquarium in perfect health, there are

certain minimum mainte-
nance requirements neces-
sary. Tank maintenance is
extremely important, and
you cannot expect to neglect
your fishes and have them
remain healthy. Feeding
your fishes on a regular basis
is not enough.

Water Changes

The single most valuable
technique in maintaining a
modified balanced aquarium
is frequent partial water
changes. If possible, 10 to15
percent changes of water

*Partial water changes should be per-
formed with some degree of regularity.*

twice a week are recommended. If time does not permit this, a 25
percent change once a week is almost as effective. When removing
old water from the aquarium, if there is any debris lying on top of
the gravel, siphon it off along with the old water. When you add
new water to the aquarium, be sure it is at the same temperature or
slightly warmer than the tank water itself. Always use a water conditioner to remove chlorine from the water. Add the water slowly to
be sure it does not uproot any plants or disturb the gravel.

Depending upon the fish load, your aquarium's filter will need to be
cleaned on a regular basis. Remove the old carbon and filter pad(s)
and throw them away, and replace them with new material (always
rinse the carbon with warm water before use). If you are making frequent partial water changes, the water quality in your aquarium
should not deteriorate.

Test Your pH!

To be on the safe side, test your pH weekly or just before changing

Overfeeding

The single most important factor that will unbalance your "modified" balanced aquarium is overfeeding. Most people love to feed their fishes, and it is not unreasonable to feed them four to six times a day. Fishes can live quite happily on two feedings a day, however, so if that is the number you have selected, feed them in the morning and evening. If you can feed them more often, feed them every four hours while the lights are on. Of course, it is recommended that the tank lights be kept on your aquarium between 12 and 16 hours a day. Should you leave the lights on constantly, you will get a bloom of algae, and the water will turn green. Also, constant light will not allow the fishes a resting or "sleep" period, and species that are not normally aggressive may become so. Yes, there are such things as "cranky" fishes!

the aquarium's water. Should you find that the water has become too acidic, it may be important to make a larger water change to bring the pH back within an acceptable range. However, please realize that some fishes will appreciate the lower pH from the start. As you advance in this hobby, you will learn which fishes prefer acidic conditions compared to those that prefer more basic, or alkaline, conditions. For the average community tank, the most widely accepted pH range measures between 6.6 to 7.2, or slightly acidic to slightly basic.

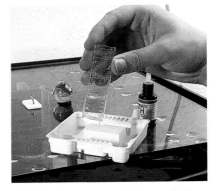

Algae Control

Another bit of tank maintenance that is strictly aesthetic in nature is algae removal or control. If algae starts to

Be sure to test your pH before and after adding fishes, performing water changes, and just for the heck of it!

Scraping algae from your aquarium's glass can be done with one of many devices. A magnetic scraper is pictured here.

grow on the glass or decorations, this may indicate that too much light may be reaching the tank and/or there are too many nutrients in your aquarium's water. Remove the algae from the glass, but leave it on the rocks for the fishes to nibble on. Water that is starting to turn green has an algal bloom in it, and this may not be healthy for the fishes. There are chemicals you can add to the tank to kill this bloom, but a large water change will usually do just as good a job as long as the bloom is not too advanced.(With water changes, you will not have to worry about the residual effect of the chemicals.) UV filters, though, are the best algae controllers.

What If Your Fishes Get Sick?

It is inevitable that no matter how good a job you do of maintaining your aquarium, at some point you will have a problem with sick or diseased fishes. This is not to be looked upon as a failure, but merely the fact that most living things deteriorate as they grow older, and older organisms tend to have more problems. If you are maintaining your water quality by frequent partial water changes and monitoring your pH, you should be able to circumvent problems for a considerable length of time. One of the ways that diseases can be brought into the aquarium is if you recently added new plants.. All new additions to the tank should be thoroughly disinfected with a strong solution of potassium permanganate before they are placed in the aquarium.

New Fishes

The introduction of new fishes is probably the most common way that problems are brought to an already established tank. Frequently, a fish will be sick, but there will be no outward manifestations of the problem. It will only gradually become apparent over a period of several days or weeks.

Parasitic Infestations

Basically, there are two types of problems that you will have to deal with when it comes to fish diseases. These are parasitic infestations and bacterial or fungal infections. Many fish parasites are visible on the body of the fish after they reach a certain stage of development or have multiplied to a sufficient extent. Once you have detected these visible spots, it is up to you to determine what they are and treat them accordingly. The most common aquarium parasite is *Ichthyophthirius multifiliis*, better known as ICK. It manifests itself by forming numerous white spots on the body and fins of the fish. It is easily cured using readily available commercial remedies.

These Oscars are affected with Ick, a common external parasite.

This Discus is suffering from the stress of collection and transport. In time, it will become strikingly beautiful.

You will find that several of the treatments used to combat parasitic infestations, such as acriflavine, contain a dye, and will discolor your water. This dye allows the hobbyist to know that the medication is present. When you are using medications, it is important that you discontinue the use of activated carbon filtration so that the medication is not absorbed by the carbon and

Fish Meds

Ask your pet shop dealer which medications are best for your particular situation. Another disease similar to ICK is "velvet," caused by the parasite *Oodinium*. This disease is a bit more difficult to cure, but it can be done if you are diligent. Again, ask your pet shop dealer what he uses.

thereby rendered ineffective. It will still be important to maintain filtration, however, so remove the carbon from your filter, and put the floss back in. (You may need to add gravel or marbles to an inside filter to hold it down.) Once you notice that the spots have disappeared for five days or more, you may consider the treatment completed, and it is then a good idea to change as much as 75 percent of the water, although a 50 percent water change is probably better.

Bacterial & Fungal Infections

Bacterial infections often become complicated by fungus. Basically, when the tank environment deteriorates to the extent that a bloom of bacteria has occurred, the bacteria attack weak fish that have open wounds and kill selected areas of flesh. Fungus soon grows on this dead flesh. If you notice small white tufts of hair-like filamentous material on your fishes, they have a fungal infection. There are many drugs available at your pet shop that will cure fungal infections. Be careful when using some drugs

This molly is a "balloon-body" type, not to be confused with one that is suffering from bloat disease.

Bacterial and fungal infections are common in fishes that have previously been wounded.

(including dyes); the packages will carry information as to whether they are safe for all types of fishes. In some cases, certain drugs may kill your plants. It is always recommended that if only one or two fishes in a community aquarium are infected, these should be removed immediately to a small treatment or hospital tank, so the drug will not have to be used in the main tank. This will save money since you will be using less medication, and it will go a long way to ensure that other fishes are not exposed to the same disease.

One of the things you might have to consider when determining what has caused a particular problem in your aquarium is the age of the fishes. Most livebearers live only two to three years, so if you have purchased mature fish initially, it is likely that they may be reaching the end of the line. This can be determined by several signs of old age, such as weight loss, subdued colors, humpbacks, and abnormal swimming motions. At this point, it might be best to remove a sick fish before it dies in the tank and causes additional problems in the community aquarium.

Your selection of fishes will be critical to the success of your aquarium, but you should not expect to make all the right decisions at first. After some time, you will learn which fishes you like and which you don't like, and you will become familiar with the disposition of each species. It is inevitable that you will want to purchase more of the fishes you like and get rid of those you do not like.

There are many excellent books on fish diseases. It is important that you get a copy as a reference guide, so you can identify the problem and its solution as soon as possible. Offering first aid to your fishes will save you more than the value of a fish disease book. It is more efficient to identify an exact problem and treat it accordingly, rather than having to constantly replace dead fish or the entire community.

Resources

MAGAZINES

Tropical Fish Hobbyist
1 T.F.H. Plaza
3rd & Union Avenues
Neptune City, NJ 07753
Phone: (732) 988-8400
E-mail: info@tfh.com
www.tfhmagazine.com

INTERNET RESOURCES

A World of Fish
www.aworldoffish.com
Aquarium Hobbyist
www.aquariumhobbyist.com
Cichlid Forum
www.cichlid-forum.com
Discus Page Holland
www.dph.nl
FINS: The Fish Information Service
http://fins.actwin.com
Fish Geeks
www.fishgeeks.com
Fish Index
www.fishindex.com
MyFishTank.Net
www.myfishtank.net
Piranha Fury
www.piranha-fury.com
Planet Catfish
www.planetcatfish.com
Tropical Resources
www.tropicalresources.net
Water Wolves
http://forums.waterwolves.com

SOCIETIES & ORGANIZATIONS

Association of Aquarists
David Davis, Membership Secretary
2 Telephone Road
Portsmouth, Hants, England
PO4 0AY
Phone: 01705 798686

British Killifish Association
Adrian Burge, Publicity Officer
E-mail: adjan@wym.u-net.com
www.bka.org.uk

Canadian Association of Aquarium Clubs
Miecia Burden, Membership Coordinator
142 Stonehenge Pl.
Kitchener, Ontario, Canada
N2N 2M7
Phone: (517) 745-1452
E-mail: mbburden@look.ca
www.caoac.on.ca

Federation of American Aquarium Societies
Jane Benes, Secretary
923 Wadsworth Street
Syracuse, NY 13208-2419
Phone: (513) 894-7289
E-mail: jbenes01@yahoo.com
www.gcca.net/faas

Goldfish Society of America
P.O. Box 551373
Fort Lauderdale, FL 33355
E-mail: info@goldfishsociety.org
www.goldfishsociety.org

International Betta Congress
Steve Van Camp, Secretary
923 Wadsworth St.
Syracuse, NY 13208
Phone: (315) 454-4792
E-mail: bettacongress@yahoo.com
www.ibcbettas.com

International Fancy Guppy Association
Rick Grigsby, Secretary
3552 West Lily Garden Lane
South Jordan, Utah 84095
Phone: (801) 694-7425
E-mail: genx632@yahoo.com
www.ifga.org

Index

Photographers:

H. Custers
B. Degen
J. Elias
W. Fink
I. Francis
R. Hagen
R. Hunziker
B. Kahl
H. Linke

O. Lucanus
H. Mayer
A. Norman
J. O'Malley
MP. & C. Piednoir
H. Piken
J. Quinn
M. Sharp
K. Tanaka

H-J. Richter
F. Rosenzweig
A. Roth
G. Schmelzer
M. Shobo
M. Smith
E. Taylor
J. Vierke
Dr. S. Weitzman